Beach Etiquette

Rules & tips for
a fun filled
Beach Day

By
Karianne Hawkins

ISBN 978-1-62806-176-5

Library of Congress Control Number 2018948418

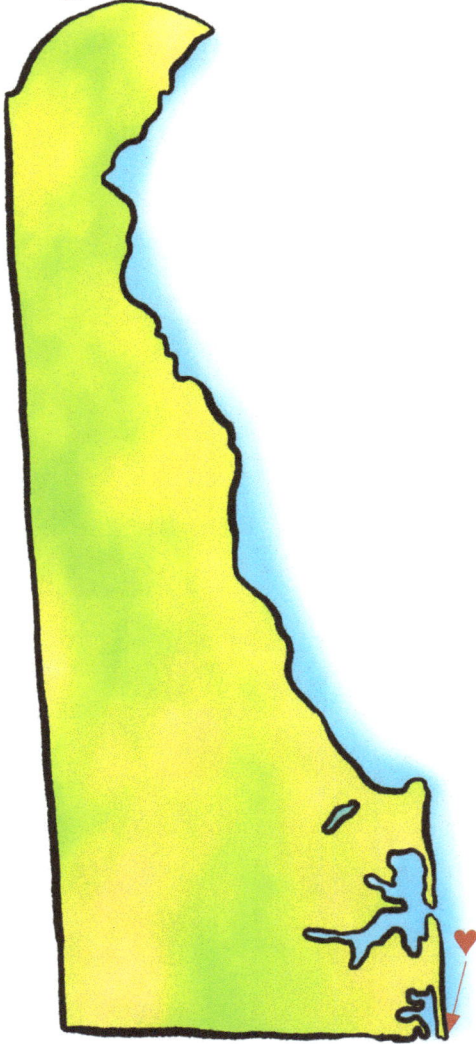

Delaware

Dedication

In memory of my dad Ralph Hawkins, miss and love you.

To my mom, sister, family and friends.

To my mom, sister Kristin & the Oster clan (Danny, Michael, Cady, Christopher & Sammy) I would not be who & where I am without all your love and support. Thank you for all the memories, support and experiences you showed and taught me along this life journey. I love you all.

Kimmie, thank you for all your help and support!

My friends & extended family, I could not have asked for a better group to surround myself with and your friendship and love mean the world to me.

Table of Contents

1. Essentials for the Beach

2 .Personal Space

3. Sun Screen

4. Sand Sensibility

5. Children

6. Ocean/Sea Creatures

7. Sand Dunes/Locals

8. Beach Parties

9. Non-Ocean Beaches

10. Manners/Etiquette

11. Leave Footprints

Essentials For The Beach

The beach is about simplicity and should be a happy place shared with friends, family, and strangers.

There are some much needed essentials for your day at the beach. Some "TIPS" are included for you to complete prior to arriving at the beach to ensure a day filled with fun, sun, and - if you're ocean bound - surf.

- **Beach Towels**

If you are in the market for towels, make sure you buy the oversized towels or beach towels specifically – unless you really want your toes in the sand!

- **Beach Chairs**

Chairs with cup-holders are especially great!

- **Umbrella**

Much needed beach essential if you get burned easily, for extremely hot days or if you need shade to take a nap

- **Sunscreens / Lip balms**

All sunscreens & Lip Balms can be applied before hitting the beach and re-applied throughout the day.

- **BABY POWDER**

TIP: Apply baby powder to skin that is sandy and it will quickly absorb moisture and the sand will fall away.

- **SAND / BEACH TOYS**

Buckets, Shovels, Rafts, Boogie & skim boards and games.

TIP: Purchase a mesh beach bag for the toys – These allow for easy clean up with sand. When you get home and the toys are dry you can shake the sand off outside.

- **COOLER**

Pack beverages, snacks, sandwiches, etc.

TIP: Preparing everything the night before is the way to go.

- **SANITIZER**

The sand may be contaminated with bacteria at levels much higher than the ocean. Use especially before eating.

• Badges/Permits

Some beaches are private and require a badge or permit on your car. Make sure you have all required materials with you because some beaches have patrol cars checking.

TIP: Pin or stick the beach's badge to your bag you take every day to the beach.

• Carts

Lugging all the essentials over to the beach can be a big issue and take a lot out of you and your back! A beach cart is a MUST have. A cart allows you to pack up all your essentials and glide across the sand.

TIP: Do Not try to wheel a wagon, stroller, etc. onto the beach, they are very hard to get through the sand. You want to buy a cart with big wheels to get across the sand with ease, they have a large capacity, are easy to handle and made especially for the beach.

- ## Wind Screen

They block the wind and sand and creates privacy. Allows you to bask in the sun without the chill of the wind. These can be purchased online or you can make your own out of burlap.

- ## Bug Spray

Great to carry with you because flies could be bad on the beach, especially if there is a land breeze.

- ## Beverages

Especially Water – It is important to stay hydrated when you spend a lot of time in the sun.

- ## Clothing

TIP: Use a hat, sunglasses, shirt or cover-up when the sun gets to be too much. These essentials are for your protection from the sun. Wear these over to the beach so you know you have them with you.

People come on the beach at different times during the day. There obviously is not a set time, but if you head over in the morning the sun is not as hot and you will get a great spot on the beach. The beach gets a bit more crowded early afternoon and people start leaving late afternoon. The best times with less traffic would be early morning and late afternoon!

Personal Space

When arriving at the beach, please look around and take into account others on the beach who have already set-up.

A lot of beaches are quite wide with more than enough room to keep a comfortable distance from others. When choosing where to stake out your territory, place all your belongings between 10-15ft away from others.

TIP: When you 'claim your ground' spread your chairs and towels out a bit further than your group would usually sit or hang out.

Avoid blocking others view of the ocean. People come to the beach to relax and observe the ocean, not to be looking through a group of others.

No one wants strangers to be part of their conversations, hear screaming kids or listen to others music.

Be aware that the tide will come in at some point during the day. Choose your personal space wisely, so you are not washed away, or, if you do have to move you are not moving on top of someone else.

TIP: Keep your cell phones, cameras and valuables in a zip lock baggy. If the water does come up unexpectedly, everything is protected.

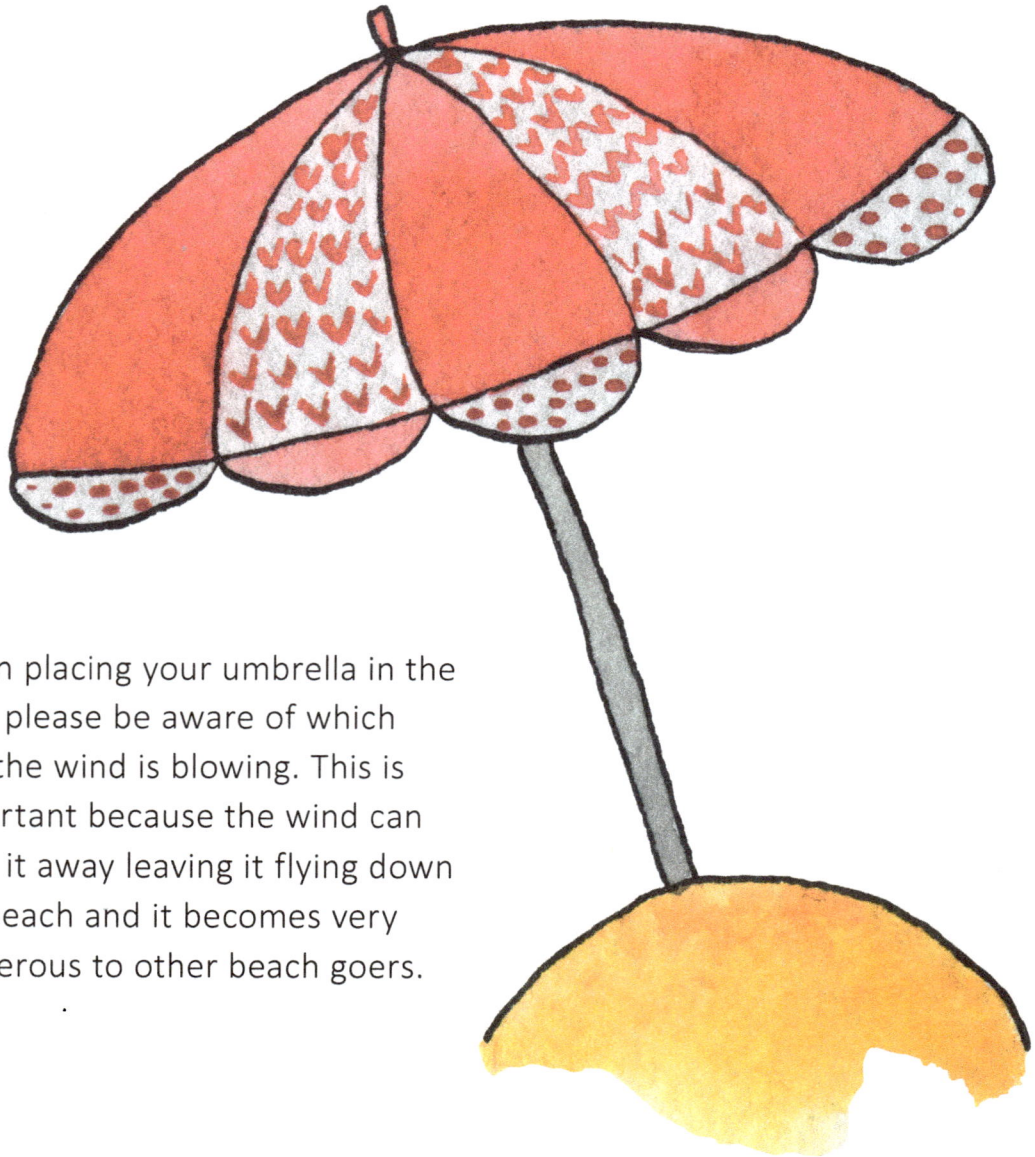

When placing your umbrella in the sand please be aware of which way the wind is blowing. This is important because the wind can blow it away leaving it flying down the beach and it becomes very dangerous to other beach goers.

.

TIP: When you have a big group going to the beach, I suggest you head to the beach early to claim your prime location! You can always set up chairs, leave and come back in a few hours.

TIP: The beaches are crowded and a good way for your friends and family to locate you is by putting something unique in your location (i.e. flag, tent, bright beach towels, or even fly a kite).

Remember: If you are that beach goer who claims good real estate early and someone is arriving late in the day and sets up shop on top of you, you have some options:

-Evaluate the area, if crowded you may have to let this one slide

-If there is no one around, request some more space before they are settled in

-You also have the option of moving if you feel uncomfortable asking them to move

maybe they will get the hint and the next time they come to the beach they will give others space

Just be considerate when picking out your territory on the beach...

Put yourself in someone else's flip flops!

Sunscreen

Sunscreens come in a variety of ways:

- Lotions/Oils
- Spray
- Toilettes
- Sunless Tanners

ALWAYS PROTECT YOUR BODY FROM THE SUN'S HARMFUL RAYS

TIP: Be aware and consider the direction the wind is blowing if you are using spray lotions on the beach. It can travel into someone else's eyes, mouth, or food. Plus, with the wind and spray lotions you may miss your skin and end up burnt.

TIP: When applying sunscreen — Make sure you apply evenly, because if you miss a spot you could end up with an uneven tan or a bad burn in the wrong spot!

Please check your bottle, toilettes or your choice of Sunless lotions for an SPF and an expiration date. Sunless lotions are the fastest way to get a tan and the fastest way to get burnt if you are not careful.

TIP: Apply sunscreen 30 minutes before heading out in the sun – also reapply throughout the day because sunscreen wears off within a few hours.

Remember that sunscreen alone does not completely protect you from the sun – if you need extra shade there are several ways to keep cool and protect your skin from the hot sun.

- -Baseball cap

- -Wide brim hat

- -Sun glasses

- -Umbrella

- -Beach tents

A fun way to make your own tent on the beach is to put two chairs back to back - leaving space in between - and drape your towels from one chair back to the other. This is great, especially for kids who like the shade!

TIP: Remember some beaches rent chairs and umbrellas – Do your research on the resort area you are visiting.

SPF sunscreens are essential to healthy living, if you happen to get burnt there are a few remedies that could help: aloe, aspirin to reduce inflammation, hydrocortisone to relieve pain and lots of fluids.

SUNBURN TREATMENT

ALOE VERA

COOL SHOWER

SUNSCREEN

DRINK WATER

MOISTURIZERS

PAIN RELIEVERS

TIP: If your eyes are sunburned you can use tea bags soaked in cold water to reduce the swelling.

TIP: There are numerous sunscreens out there that are waterproof, sweat-resistant as well as zinc oxides made of fun bright colors as well.

Sand Sensibility

The sand is what we cannot wait to feel between our toes, dig your hands into, and place your chair into. It's the 1st sign you are actually, really, finally at the beach.

We also need to be smart about the sand while others are around.

When arriving at the beach, if the sand is not super-hot, take off your flip-flops or sandals- Walking with them on in the sand is pretty much a sure guarantee that you'll be flipping sand up.

TIP: If the sand is very hot leave on your flip flops and make a beeline for the colder sand, which is by the water!! You could also use your towel to walk on – carefully!

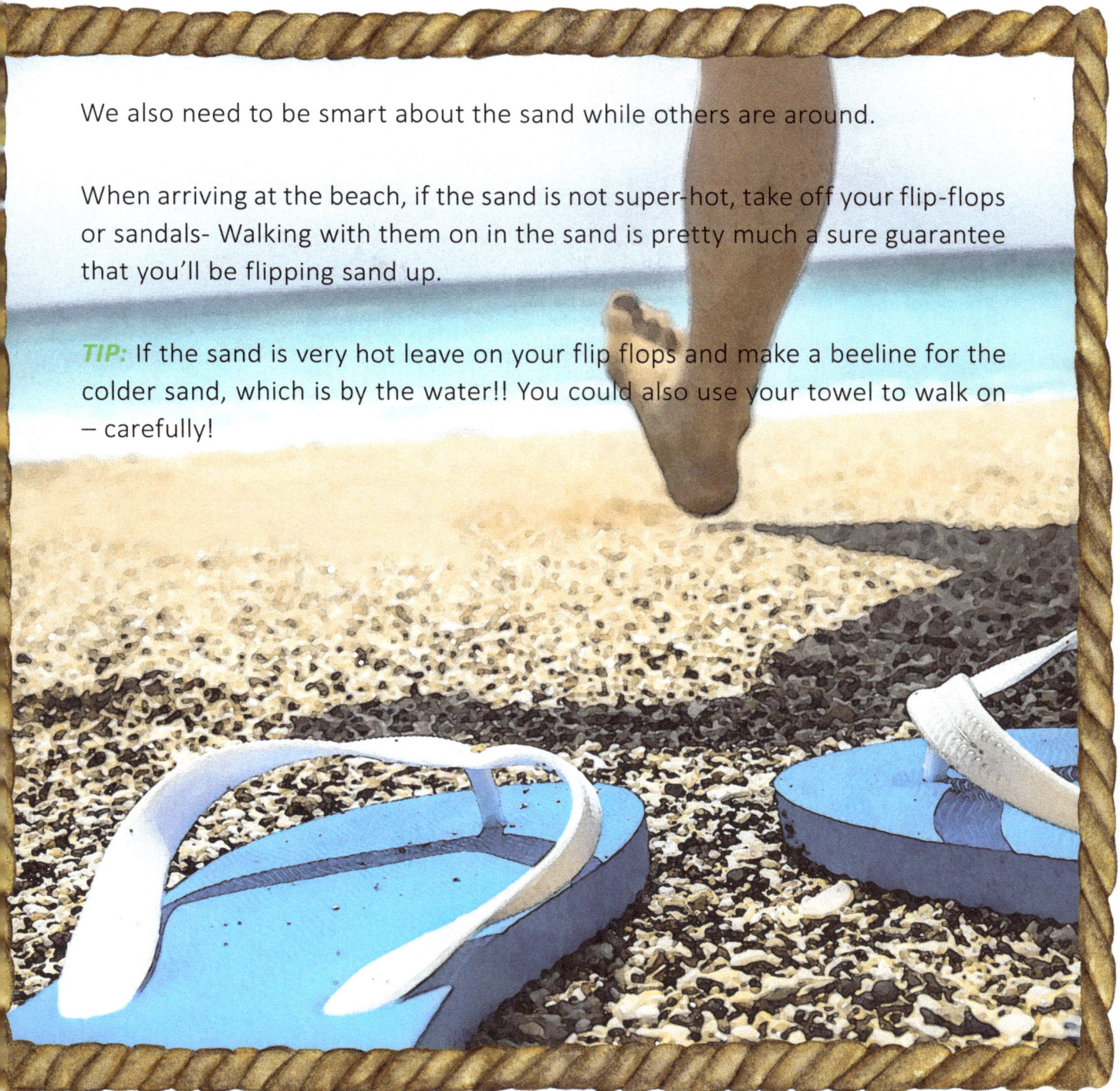

No throwing or kicking sand

Don't walk too close to others on the beach or through another group of people.

Don't shake your towel or blankets out too close to others

TIP: Make sure you know which way the wind is blowing before you shake towels out. You can also walk away from your group towards the dunes and shake them out.

One of the worst things is to have a sandy kid, sand stuck to you or sandy feet going into your house:

TIP: Baby Powder – Carry it in your beach bag at all times!!!

SAND SAFETY: The sand can be pretty harmless, but burying people in the sand and hanging out in large dug out holes can carry dangers for children. The sand can be very unstable and slide down trapping a child. Please watch your kids closely and play safe.

There are numerous things for kids/adults to do in the sand that are fun and entertaining:

-Build sand castles

-Collect shells

-Play games (volleyball, throwing a ball, ladder ball, smash ball, corn hole)

Children

Children grow up looking
forward to the beach
every summer where many
lifelong memories
are made.

Kids are always excited when arriving at the beach, but you need to make sure there is NO running onto the beach around others. The sand flies everywhere.

TIP: Wearing boat shoes in the water is a good idea with the potential of sharp objects on the ocean floor.

Follow all directions and instructions from the lifeguards. Pay attention to flags and signs that warn you about the tide and marine life posted on their stands.

Usually these are the standard flag meanings; please check in with your lifeguard for your particular beach:

BEACH WARNING FLAGS TYPES

NO SWIMMING
(high hazard)

SWIMMING AREA
(with lifeguards)

SURFING AREA
(no swimming)

CAUTION
(medium hazard)

DANGEROUS
MARINE LIFE

NO WATERCRAFTS
& SURFBOARDS

SAFE TO SWIM
(calm conditions)

WARNING
(dirty water or air)

VERY DANGEROUS
(water closed to public use)

DIVING
(in progress)

ABSENCE OF FLAG
DOES NOT ASSURE
SAFE WATER!

-Double red flags – Water closed

-Red flag – High surf-currents

-Yellow flag – Moderate surf & current

-Green flag – Calm surf

-Purple flag – Dangerous marine life

Lifeguards are not at the beach to be babysitters – Keep an eye on your own children so they are not disturbing other beach goers.

TIP: When swimming take a buddy with you, or, when in doubt – don't go out!

When digging holes, do not have your kids dig in front of other 'beach-goers' spots– you do not want to cause injuries.

Also see 'Sand Safety' for more information on how digging holes can be dangerous and why you should keep an eye on your kids.

No Screaming or yelling. There are many other beach goers that come to the beach for a relaxing day - not a day at the playground!

Ocean and Sea Creatures

You're at the beach to enjoy a soothing and calming atmosphere as well as to cool off and have some fun.

SEA LIFE

But beware: marine life can be dangerous. Make yourself aware of the Ocean once arriving and settling in. (Rip currents, sea creatures and fishing areas)

TIP: Depending on the beach you go to there may be lifeguards and may not. If there are lifeguards on your beach they usually will have information on back of their stand stating issues that are occurring that day on the beach.

TIP: Never go out farther than you can swim.

The ocean houses many sea creatures and plants and is directly impacted by pollution. Please don't dump waste or litter.

Chances are you will encounter crabs, sand crabs, fish, jelly fish, dolphin, horse shoe crabs, turtles and other living animals and plants at the beach. Make yourself aware and observe and please DO NOT remove them from their home. You wouldn't want to be taken away from what you are used to – would you?

TIP: Jelly Fish sting — It's a good idea to keep items used on stings with you when going to the beach (vinegar, meat tenderizer, and ibuprofen). Please make sure if you get stung that you are not allergic. If not, first rinse the sting off in the ocean — salt water is best. Also, believe it or not, the urban legend that says if you urinate on the sting it relieves the pain, that's FALSE!!!! It actually makes it worse.

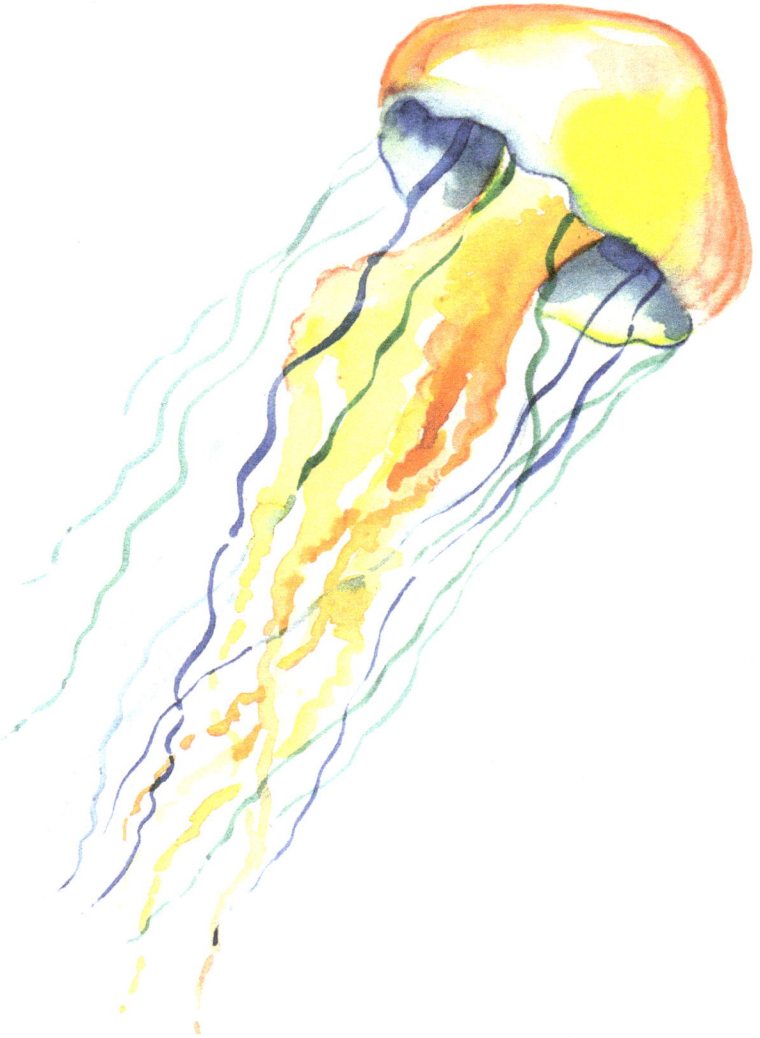

Sand Dunes and Locals

The Dunes are there for a reason.

They help preserve and provide shelter for the wildlife and protect the surrounding area from beach erosion.

KEEP
OFF
THE
DUNE

Follow the marked paths to the beach... they are there for a reason.

It's illegal to cut, break or destroy any sea plants,
beach grass or sand fencing.

These all protect the locals who live year round at a beach community
against flooding and erosion.

Beach Parties

Every day is a party at the beach!! The beach puts people in a good mood and if you are planning a beach party with friends and family this should be the most relaxing party to plan.

The most important part of the party is already in place – the beach itself. The "Essentials for the Beach" are a must. Refer back to Chapter 1.

If it is a get together on the beach with friends/family no formal invite is necessary (word of mouth could be enough), but if it's a celebration/theme a formal invite would be recommended. Not all beaches are the same. One may be good for the surf and sun, but not right for a beach party.

TIP: Research the rules and regulations for the beaches in your beach community.

If it happens to rain have a back-up plan in place – We are dealing with Mother Nature.

Timing of party – Is it an all-day event, do you want to have a combo of the sun, sunset, bonfire?

Communication is key to any beach party because each of your friends/ family have something to contribute. One friend may have fun beach games (ladder ball, corn hole, Frisbee, etc.) and one may have a big cooler to hold a lot of drinks and food.

TIP: Make it Potluck – everyone brings a snack to share amongst the group (This is communicated with everyone in the group on what each person is bringing).

TIP: Someone in your group is bound to have a portable grill, find that person!! If no one does, buy one. So much fun to grill burgers and hot dogs on the beach!

If you are having a 'Celebration Beach Party' all the work is in the hands of the host!

TIP: For an invite a postcard with a picture of the area on the front and all the details on the back would be cute.

Most celebration parties on the beach (graduation, wedding or birthday) don't need all the decorations you would in your house.

Just remember, as the host, you need to have the essentials that are a MUST for a beach party all set up when your guests arrive.

Non-Ocean Beaches

While many people spend their vacation and summer days on the beach at the ocean, there are also many who vacation and live on the beautiful lakes, rivers and bays across our country. A lot of the etiquette advice and tips given in the previous chapters is also very important when planning a fun-filled day on a lake, river or bay.

A day on the lake, river or bay can be very similar to days on the beach so refer back to the earlier chapters when planning your day.

Much like the beaches there are also rules and regulations that preserve and protect. Do Not take creatures or drift wood. Take only pictures and leave waves!

One of the major differences from the ocean is activities on the water. Motor sports are a huge part of vacationing on the lakes, rivers and bays. There are a lot more motor activities and non-motor activities (wave running, boating, fishing kayaking, paddle boarding) happening.

TIP: When going out on the water it is always important to check your local weather conditions for the day.

TIP: There are many restrictions and rules for boating – Please be aware of these and be considerate of fellow boaters on the water and wear your lifejackets.

TIP: When you are on the water, please be aware of "No Wake" signs when close to the shoreline. Respect these signs, as they protect the locals' docks from being destroyed and the beach from shoreline erosion. The shoreline is very important on the lakes, rivers and bays.

TIP: Residents living on the shoreline need to be cautious about getting fertilizers and cleaners in the water. We need to keep our water clean.

Manners:

The beach is a different world, with many different ways to entertain yourself.

You can be a sun bather, work-out in the sand, fish, play beach games, water sports, build castles, observe others around you, read a good book, enjoy your group's company or simply take a stroll down the beach collecting shells.

The beach has a lot to offer everyone, but the common factor with so many different personalities in one place at one time, is respecting your fellow beach bums!

Music/Voice- Keep it for your ears only.

Don't mess with other people's stuff.

Sports/Exercising on the beach - Take your activities away from where everyone is sitting or closer to the Dunes. No one wants to be hit by a frisbee, football, beach balls, etc....

PDA (Public Displays of Affection) You're in public not your home. Be respectful.

Sunbathing – Please keep your suits on!

Beach Appeal - Well let's just say Speedos are no longer in! Leave them for sunbathing in private.

Do not joke around unless you are hurt or drowning in the water – that is serious business.

Be thoughtful in the water (No crazy splashing while others are around, dunking, yelling and maintain control of your boogie board straps and other water toys)

WARNING

NO VEHICLES BEYOND THIS POINT WITHOUT VALID DELAWARE SURF FISHING VEHICLE PERMIT

- SURF FISHING EQUIPMENT REQUIRED AT ALL TIMES
- MUST BE ACTIVELY ENGAGED IN SURF FISHING AT ALL TIMES

- PETS MUST BE ON A LEASH AT ALL TIMES
- KEEP OFF DUNES AND BEACH GRASS

DELAWARE DIVISION OF PARKS AND RECREATION

LEASH LAW
STRICTLY
ENFORCED

SINGLE FILE PARKING ONLY
BETWEEN
OCEAN AND DUNE

Make sure all wrappers, bags etc. are secure and nothing is blowing away polluting the beaches. NO glass on the beach.

Do Not let your dogs or kids run loose.

Dogs always on leash if you're on a beach which allows dogs.

NO feeding the Seagulls

Many people think that it is harmless to feed them or throw away the last bite of the sandwich or last chip. It's not – please be respectful of others on the beach, birds swarm to food and arrive almost immediately. Within minutes, dozens of birds can completely take over your space! They are a nuisance, noisy and can be aggressive.

DO NOT FEED THE SEAGULLS

Footprints

Carry out more than what you came with.

Take only photographs and memories.

Leave only Footprints.

www.ingramcontent.com/pod-product-compliance
Lightning Source LLC
Chambersburg PA
CBHW041430270326